GIRLFRIEND TO GIRLFRIEND

A Journey of Faith, Friendship, and Finding Yourself Again

Foreword

Rev. Dr. Candace Kelly

FLORENTINE SHIRLEY

Girlfriend to Girlfriend

A Journey of Faith, Friendship, and Finding Yourself Again

Copyright © 2025 Florentine Shirley
All rights reserved.

Printed and bound in the United States of America

Published by Cole Publishing

Library of Congress
Cataloging-in-Publication Data
ISBN: 979-8-9885825-9-5

Cole Publishing
4067 Hardwick Street #282
Lakewood, CA 90712

Email: Colepublishing2000@gmail.com
Book Cover Design by Cole Publishing Company

For Book Orders:
Contact us at Cole Publishing Company
www.ColePublishing.org

Cole Publishing

CONTENTS

DEDICATION

This book is lovingly dedicated to my Lord and Savior, who has been with me through every season of life and its many, many challenges. Through it all, I have learned that with God, all things are possible.

It is through the faith, hope, love, and encouragement I have received from God's people that I have been strengthened. For years, this book has been a desire in my heart—a dream planted by God Himself, who also gave me the gifts to bring it to life.

I am deeply grateful for the opportunity to share these gifts with others. May this offering bring comfort, inspiration, and the reminder that God's love never fails.

ACKNOWLEDGMENTS

First and foremost, I give all honor and glory to God, who made this book possible. Without His divine guidance, sustaining grace, and unconditional love, none of this would have come to life. He has been faithful through every step of this journey, and I am truly humbled and grateful.

"With God all things are possible."

MATTHEW 19:26

I would like to extend heartfelt thanks to a dear and talented friend, Minister of Music William "Bill" Marshall. It was through his kindness and connection that I was introduced to the remarkable Rev. Dr. Candace Cole-Kelly. Dr. Kelly has lovingly guided me through this beautiful spiritual journey of creating this book. Her unwavering support, spiritual wisdom, and sincere love for God have been an invaluable blessing to me.

Dr. Candace Kelly, your leadership, friendship, and sisterhood have been heaven-sent. I love you for the person that you are—gracious, wise, and full of God's light. I am so deeply appreciative of your mentorship and the genuine love you share.

"And I will give you shepherds after my own heart, who will feed you with knowledge and understanding."

JEREMIAH 3:15

To Rev. Dr. Larry Campbell and First Lady Melinda Campbell, thank you both for believing in me from the very beginning—when this book was just a dream in my heart. Your encouragement, prayers, and genuine support have meant the world to me.

A special thank you as well to Dr. Laura Young Sampson for her continuous encouragement and thoughtful words that kept me moving forward. You've been a light along this path.

"Therefore encourage one another and build one another up, just as you are doing."

1 THESSALONIANS 5:11

To my beloved sons, Jason and Joshua—thank you for being a constant source of love and strength throughout the years. Your friendship, patience, and belief in me have been a steady reminder of God's grace.

"Children are a heritage from the Lord, offspring a reward from him."

PSALM 127:3

I would also like to thank the amazing staff at Cole Publishing Company & Consultants for their creative touch in bringing forth my first book with excellence, elegance, and eloquence. Thank you for all that you do behind the scenes to uplift voices and visions with professionalism and purpose.

"And let the beauty of the Lord our God be upon us,
and establish the work of our hands for us."

PSALM 90:17

To everyone who has walked alongside me, spoken a word of encouragement, or prayed for me during this process—thank you. May God bless you as richly as you've blessed me.

"I thank my God every time I remember you."

PHILIPPIANS 1:3

With love and deep gratitude,
Florentine Shirley

FOREWORD

There are moments in every woman's life when she pauses—sometimes in pain, sometimes in joy, and sometimes in quiet reflection—wondering, *"Who am I now, and where is God leading me?"* It is in these tender spaces that the gentle voice of a friend, a sister, or a spiritual guide becomes the balm we need. *Girlfriend to Girlfriend* is exactly that—an invitation into a sacred conversation between hearts, where faith is strengthened, friendship is rekindled, and the soul is reminded of its worth.

Florentine Shirley, a woman of unwavering faith and enduring grace, has penned this beautiful collection of poetry and spiritual reflection from the wellspring of her own journey with God. Her words are not just written; they are lived. With decades of experience in ministry, community service, and personal triumphs through adversity, Florentine writes with a voice seasoned by compassion and steeped in wisdom.

This book is more than poetry—it is a discipleship tool, a devotional companion, and a sister-to-sister lifeline for every woman seeking to rediscover herself in Christ. Whether you're walking through heartbreak, celebrating a new beginning, or simply needing a quiet moment of truth, each page draws you into the presence of a God who heals, restores, and calls you beloved.

As you journey through these verses, may you laugh, cry, reflect, and most importantly—remember who you are and whose you are. Let this be your reminder that even when life feels uncertain, the love of God, shared from girlfriend to girlfriend, is a steady and unshakable foundation.

Rev. Dr. Candace Kelly

President and CEO
Cole Publishing Company & Consultatnts

FRIEND

"Friend" — a word we often use with ease,
Yet one of truth is seldom found with peace
Acceptance, caring, honesty, and love,
Are sacred gifts, bestowed from God above.
When we reflect His heart in word and deed,
We become a friend to those in need.
For kindness born from deep within the soul,
Is how God's blessings overflow and roll.
I've met someone so precious, rare, and true—
A child of God, with love in all they do.
One who listens, gives, and always shares,
With gentle strength and heartfelt prayers.
And so, within the quiet of my heart,
I thank the Lord for what you truly are—
A faithful friend, a gift without end,
A soul I cherish... whom I call **friend**.

What qualities make someone a true friend in God's eyes?

◌\ Proverbs 17:17

"A friend loves at all times, and a brother is born for a time of adversity."

Reflection:
Am I offering consistent love and support to the people in my life, even when it's inconvenient or hard?

How do your friendships influence your walk with God?

◌\ Proverbs 13:20

"Walk with the wise and become wise, for a companion of fools suffers harm."

Reflection:
Are my friends helping me grow spiritually, or pulling me away from God's purpose for my life?

In what ways are you being a Christ-like friend to others?

◌\ John 15:12-13

"My command is this: Love each other as I have loved you. Greater love has no one than this: to lay down one's life for one's friends."

Reflection:
How can I show sacrificial love, grace, and encouragement to someone close to me this week?

A KISS

A kiss—so small, yet deeply profound,
What might it mean, as it gently goes 'round?
It could hold a thousand things unsaid—
A longing for love, a prayer gently spread.

It might be a whisper of gratitude or grace,
A gesture of friendship, a soft embrace.
A kiss can echo laughter and delight,
A simple act that makes burdens light.

It may soothe wounds hidden deep inside,
Bring healing where silent sorrows abide.
Whether placed on forehead, hand, or cheek,
It speaks when words are too fragile to speak.

A kiss is more than affection displayed—
It's a holy reminder that someone stayed.
In the act of caring, it finds its place—
A tender reflection of God's own grace.

What is the intention behind the kiss I give or receive—love, respect, betrayal, or reverence?

⌒\ Luke 22:48 (NIV)

"But Jesus asked him, 'Judas, are you betraying the Son of Man with a kiss?'"

Reflection: How can we be more mindful of our motives and the hearts behind our actions, even in something as simple as a kiss?

How can I honor others with pure affection and godly expressions of care?

Romans 16:16 (NIV)

"Greet one another with a holy kiss."

Reflection: What are practical ways I can greet or care for others with holiness, especially in a culture that often misuses physical expressions?

Do my acts of affection point others to the compassion and love of Christ?

⌒\ Romans 12:9 (ESV)

"Let love be genuine. Abhor what is evil; hold fast to what is good."

Reflection: In what ways can I express love in a manner that is authentic, godly, and healing to others?

CLOSENESS GIVEN BY GOD

It's truly a wonder, a beautiful thing,
To watch how our friendship continues to spring.
Like seeds in the soil, deeply rooted and strong,
A connection divine that's been growing all along.

I'm deeply grateful to our Father above,
For blessing me with your God-given love.
You give so freely—no judgment, no gain,
Just kindness and care that helps soften life's pain.

In a world where self often reigns supreme,
Your selfless heart feels like a dream.
This bond we share, pure and sincere,
Is something only God could engineer.

He knows our needs before we say a word,
And answers in ways that seem unheard.
This closeness we hold, not built on show,
Is a sacred tie that continues to grow.

It's not about titles or what people see—
It's about God's Spirit dwelling in you and me.
So in His perfect will, we'll walk day by day,
Giving Him glory as we trust and pray.

How do you experience God's closeness in times of joy and sorrow?

ᘒ Psalm 34:18 (NIV)

"The Lord is close to the brokenhearted and saves those who are crushed in spirit."

Reflection: Reflect on a time when you felt God's nearness during a difficult season. How did His presence comfort or guide you?

How does God use relationships with others to demonstrate His love and nearness?

ᘒ Ecclesiastes 4:9-10 (NLT)

"Two people are better off than one, for they can help each other succeed. If one person falls, the other can reach out and help."

Reflection: Can you identify a friendship or relationship in which you've seen God's love clearly? How does that bond reflect His character?

What does it mean to abide in God's closeness daily, and how can we deepen that connection?

ᘒ John 15:4 (ESV)

"Abide in me, and I in you. As the branch cannot bear fruit by itself... neither can you, unless you abide in me."

Reflection: What practices help you stay close to God? In what ways do you need to invite Him into more areas of your life?

BE ENCOURAGED

I'm here to lift your heart and bring a smile,
Even if just for a little while.
I want to help ease the weight you bear,
So your healing begins with love and care.

God has placed me in your life today,
To walk beside you along the way.
Remember always—keep this in view:
God deeply loves and sees you through.

Each prayer I whisper is sent with grace,
Believing God will meet you in this place.
So lift your head—don't look behind,
Peace and hope you're sure to find.

Stand in faith, be brave, be true—
Be encouraged... Jesus loves you.

What does it mean to find strength in the Lord during difficult times?

◯\ Isaiah 40:31

"But those who hope in the Lord will renew their strength. They will soar on wings like eagles; they will run and not grow weary, they will walk and not be faint."

Reflection: How can I actively renew my strength by placing my hope in God today?

How can I become a source of encouragement to others in their time of need?

◯\ 1 Thessalonians 5:11

"Therefore encourage one another and build each other up, just as in fact you are doing."

Reflection: Who around me needs a word of encouragement, and how can I uplift them with love and compassion?

What truths from God's Word can I cling to when I feel discouraged or overwhelmed?

◯\ Joshua 1:9

"Have I not commanded you? Be strong and courageous. Do not be afraid; do not be discouraged, for the Lord your God will be with you wherever you go."

Reflection: What promise from scripture brings me peace and reminds me of God's constant presence?

YOUR SMILE

As time moved on and pressures passed,
That beautiful smile returned at last.
A smile that shines from deep within—
It tells me your healing has begun again.

Oh, how my heart rejoices to see
That joy return so visibly.
For there was a time it hid away,
But now it brightens up each day.

I thank our God, so kind and true,
For hearing the prayers lifted for you.
So keep on smiling—don't let it fade,
God's blessings are coming, perfectly laid.

He's lifting you up, making you strong,
Just hold on, it won't be long.
And as you smile from day to day,
Remember—God has made the way.

How can your smile reflect the joy and healing God is doing in your life?

ᅅ Proverbs 15:13 (NIV)

"A happy heart makes the face cheerful, but heartache crushes the spirit."

Reflection: In what ways is God restoring joy in your heart? How can your smile become a witness of His work in you?

How does gratitude for answered prayers change your outlook and attitude?

ᅅ Philippians 4:6-7 (NLT)

"Don't worry about anything; instead, pray about everything... Then you will experience God's peace, which exceeds anything we can understand."

Reflection: What prayers has God answered for you recently? How do those moments fuel a grateful heart and a joyful countenance?

What does it mean to trust that God has 'made the way' in your life journey?

ᅅ Isaiah 43:19 (ESV)

"Behold, I am doing a new thing... I will make a way in the wilderness and rivers in the desert."

Reflection: In what area of your life do you need to trust God's unseen path? How can your smile be a declaration of that trust?

GOD SENT

In all God's ways, I see His care,
For in my life, He's always aware.
Of every desire and each deep need,
He fulfills them all with holy speed.

Through days of toil and dark despair,
I feel His love—it's always there.
The things He mends, one by one,
Before I even ask—they're done.

He places angels along our way,
To guide us through each troubled day.
With bonds divine, only God can weave,
I'm grateful more than you'd believe.

Yes, God-sent souls walk by my side,
To bring me peace and hope inside.
They make today brighter than the past—
With love and grace that truly last.

Who has God "sent" into your life during a time of need, and how did their presence reflect His love and care?

◊ Psalm 34:18

"The Lord is near to the brokenhearted and saves the crushed in spirit."

Reflection: Think about a time when someone showed up at just the right moment. How did their presence or words remind you of God's awareness of your pain?

Are you willing to be a "God-sent" person to someone else?
How might God use you to encourage or strengthen another?

◊ Galatians 6:2

"Carry each other's burdens, and in this way you will fulfill the law of Christ."

Reflection: What does it look like to be available and sensitive to the Holy Spirit's leading when others are hurting?

Do you recognize the hand of God in the people He places in your path?

◊ James 1:17

"Every good and perfect gift is from above, coming down from the Father of the heavenly lights..."

Reflection: How might your perspective change if you viewed certain friendships or encounters as divine appointments rather than coincidences?

THANKING GOD FOR CARING

Don't think for a moment that I cannot see
The enormity of all you do for me.
Oh yes, I am grateful—so deeply aware,
It speaks volumes about your heart and care.

I'm thanking God, with eyes opened wide,
For His mercy, His love, forever by my side.
Not only care—but far more in store,
Is hidden in His divine resources, and more.

For God's perfect love casts out all fear,
Just let Him touch you—He's always near.
To heal the wounds that brought you pain,
And fill your soul with joy again.

So please, unlock your heart, and share with me
The dreams, the hopes of all you long "to be."
You won't be disappointed—you will see,
Though trust is hard... I ask, please trust in me.

How do you recognize God's care and provision in your daily life?

◌\ Philippians 4:19

"And my God will supply every need of yours according to His riches in glory in Christ Jesus.

Reflection: reflect on a time when God provided for you in a way that made you feel seen and loved. How did you respond?

What fears or wounds are you still holding onto that God is inviting you to release to Him?

◌\ 1 John 4:18

"There is no fear in love. But perfect love drives out fear..."

Reflection: In what areas of your life do you need to let God's love heal and replace fear?

Are there people in your life God has sent to show His care for you? Have you thanked Him for them?

◌\ James 1:17

"Every good and perfect gift is from above, coming down from the Father of the heavenly lights..."

Reflection: Who has shown you love, support, or encouragement recently? How might you express your gratitude to them and to God?

ESPECIALLY FOR YOU

Remember not too long ago,
I wrote a poem—or maybe two—
That spoke of encouragement God sent
Through me, especially for you.

I hope you still remember this:
God deeply cares how you feel.
As a friend, He placed me in your life
To help you cope and heal.

With all of life's challenges
You face from day to day,
I'm here to listen to your heart
And help in every way.

No matter what the hour,
When you need someone who'll care,
My ears are always open—
Patiently, I'll be there.

To help release the tension
Or stress that comes your way,
Sometimes it helps to speak it out
And let the burdens sway.

Please don't ever think you're bothering me,
Or that your pain is mine to dread.
It's my joy—and divine assignment—
To help bring peace instead.

So always remember, and never doubt
What a true friend you have in me.
With prayer, and strength from God above,
You will walk in hope—and be free.

ONLY YOU

I'm happy now—because of you,
My life is not the same.
You came along and filled my heart
With joy I can't explain.

For many years, I walked around
With pain that gripped my soul,
But then you entered my broken life
And gently made me whole.

I'm smiling now, it's all because
Of your sweet, tender ways.
It only took the gift of you
To brighten all my days.

Who has God used in your life to bring healing and joy?

◯\ James 1:17 (NIV)

"Every good and perfect gift is from above, coming down from the Father of the heavenly lights..."

Reflection: Think about the people or moments God has placed in your life that brought comfort and restoration. How did they reflect God's love to you?

In what ways has God restored your brokenness and brought light to your darkness?

◯\ Psalm 147:3 (ESV)

"He heals the brokenhearted and binds up their wounds."

Reflection: Consider how God met you during a difficult time. What has changed in you because of His healing?

How can you show appreciation to those who have been a light in your life?

◯\ 1 Thessalonians 5:11 (NIV)

"Encourage one another and build each other up, just as in fact you are doing."

Reflection: Are you intentional about expressing gratitude to the people God has used to bless you? How can you be that same light to someone else?

YOU & ME

I wonder how it might have been,
If we had met way back then.
Who's to say what we might see—
It could've been magic, just you and me.

But why look back on yesteryears,
When what we share now is crystal clear?
Though life once took us separate ways,
Time has gently brought us to these days.

Together again, for however long,
I'll cherish each moment as we move along.
To me, you're special—yes, it's true,
I treasure every second spent with you.

So sweet, so kind—just what I need,
It's a beautiful bond, planted like a seed.
And now it blooms so naturally—
It's really quite lovely... just you & me.

How can we recognize God's timing in relationships that reconnect or begin later in life?

ᔕ Ecclesiastes 3:1 (NIV)

"There is a time for everything, and a season for every activity under the heavens."

Reflection: How have you seen God's perfect timing play out in your own relationships?

What qualities should we cherish and nurture in someone we love and care for deeply?

ᔕ 1 Corinthians 13:4-7 (NIV)

"Love is patient, love is kind... It always protects, always trusts, always hopes, always perseveres."

Reflection: Which aspects of love do you find easiest to give—and which ones do you feel God is helping you grow in?

How can mutual appreciation and kindness strengthen emotional bonds in our lives?

ᔕ Ephesians 4:32 (NIV)

"Be kind and compassionate to one another, forgiving each other, just as in Christ God forgave you."

Reflection: In what ways can you show more intentional kindness and gratitude to someone special in your life?

AS I SEE YOU

There is a light that shines within
The deepest part of you—
It's sensitive, compassionate, caring,
And even loving too.

There is also a quiet strength
You carry deep inside,
A secret place within yourself
Where you often go to hide.

You're always pondering, thinking through,
How you hope and wish things would go—
But talk to the Lord, trust Him fully,
And He will make it so.

He will lead, guide, and protect you
In all you do and say,
For God has a plan and purpose—
Yes, He will make the way.

So always stay encouraged,
Stand strong, and keep the faith.
For one day soon, you will see—
Everything will be in its proper place.

How can I cultivate the light and compassion that shines from within me?

◌\ Matthew 5:16

"In the same way, let your light shine before others, that they may see your good deeds and glorify your Father in heaven."

What areas of my life do I need to trust God with more, knowing that He has a plan and purpose for me?

◌\ Proverbs 3:5-6

"Trust in the Lord with all your heart and lean not on your own understanding; in all your ways submit to Him, and He will make your paths straight."

How can I encourage others to stay strong in their faith and trust God's timing?

◌\ 1 Thessalonians 5:11

"Therefore encourage one another and build each other up, just as in fact you are doing."

STANDING IN FAITH

In the Lord's arms, we all must stay,
There is peace and rest to calm our way.
Just walk in faith and don't let go,
No matter the ways, the wind might blow.

Your walk of faith, some don't understand,
Although you know, you are in the Lord's hands.
He will guide and keep you in all your ways,
To establish your going from day to day.

So, stay encouraged and don't look down,
Just keep standing strong, and more strength will be found.
In all our ways, in faith, we must stand on His Word,
And rest assured, your every power will be heard!
"In the name of Jesus Christ."

How can we maintain our faith when we face challenges that others may not understand?

෴ 2 Corinthians 5:7

"For we walk by faith, not by sight."

What does it mean to stand firm in the Lord's strength, even when circumstances seem overwhelming?

෴ Ephesians 6:10

"Finally, be strong in the Lord and in the strength of His might."

How can we find peace and rest in God's presence when we are struggling in our faith?

෴ Matthew 11:28-30

"Come to me, all who labor and are heavy laden, and I will give you rest. Take my yoke upon you, and learn from me, for I am gentle and lowly in heart, and you will find rest for your souls. For my yoke is easy, and my burden is light."

ENCOURAGEMENT

There comes a time, sometime or another,
When encouragement we need from a sister or brother.
Sometimes we have to encourage ourselves,
'Cause from where we look, there is no help.

No matter what happens or how things run,
Remember Christ loves you, He's God's only Son.
Whatever you endeavor to do,
Let no one discourage that drive in you.

Some days are long and harder than others,
But just keep striving, it is not much further.
Some people sometimes, they cannot understand,
So I say unto you...

How can you encourage others during difficult times, and why is it important to offer encouragement from a place of faith?

❧ 1 Thessalonians 5:11 (NIV)

"Therefore encourage one another and build each other up, just as in fact you are doing."

When you feel discouraged, what can you remind yourself about God's promises and how He strengthens you in times of need?

❧ Psalm 34:18 (NIV)

"The Lord is close to the brokenhearted and saves those who are crushed in spirit."

How can you encourage yourself in the Lord when challenges arise, and how does His Word provide strength?

❧ Philippians 4:13 (NIV)

"I can do all this through him who gives me strength."

DIVINE GUIDANCE

Sometimes in life, decisions are hard to make,
If for no other reason than fear of mistake.
But if you ask God to guide your life,
Your chosen outcome will always be right.

For the perfect love of God casts out all fear,
Just ask for His will in your life to appear.
For in His way, there is no strife, fear, or pain,
If you let Him guide you, only joy will remain.

Deep within, we all want, need, and desire love,
But real love comes only through God above.
So, if you let Him guide you, one step at a time,
Try to open your heart—oh! Yes, it is time.

For the Great I AM, who will talk to you,
To lead and guide you safely through!

How can you discern God's guidance in your decisions, especially when faced with uncertainty?

૭\ Proverbs 3:5-6 (NIV)

"Trust in the Lord with all your heart and lean not on your own understanding; in all your ways submit to him, and he will make your paths straight."

What role does prayer play in receiving God's guidance in difficult situations?

૭\ James 1:5 (NIV)

"If any of you lacks wisdom, let him ask of God, who gives to all liberally and without reproach, and it will be given to him."

How can we ensure that we are following God's will rather than our own desires?

૭\ Romans 12:2 (NIV)

"Do not conform to the pattern of this world, but be transformed by the renewing of your mind. Then you will be able to test and approve what God's will is—his good, pleasing, and perfect will."

ONE STEP AT A TIME

To take one step, one step at a time,
Can ease and heal a troubled mind.
Sometimes we forget where our help comes from,
It comes from God who reigns from above.

We lean on our flesh, which is oh! so weak,
But if we trust in Him, our life is complete.
Filled with love, joy, peace, and rest,
If you trust in Him, He will give you His best.

Oh! I'm a sinner and not worthy to ask!
But He sits there waiting to help with each task.
It takes one step, one step at a time,
Just ask Him, you'll see, and it will be thine.

No matter what we say, or what we do,
We are all God's children, and He is waiting for you.

How can you trust in God's guidance, one step at a time, when facing difficult decisions or challenges?

❧ Proverbs 3:5-6

"Trust in the Lord with all your heart and lean not on your own understanding; in all your ways submit to him, and he will make your paths straight."

What are some areas in your life where you may be relying too much on your own strength rather than God's strength, and how can you surrender those to Him for His guidance?

❧ Isaiah 40:29

"He gives strength to the weary and increases the power of the weak."

Reflection: Reflect on how taking one step at a time in obedience to God's will can lead to peace and fulfillment.

What does it mean for you to trust that God will provide His best for you, even when the path ahead is unclear?

❧ Matthew 6:33

"But seek first his kingdom and his righteousness, and all these things will be given to you as well."

PRAISE AMIDST CHALLENGE

Within my life, I see His care,
His grace and mercy are standing there
To carry me through each challenge of life—
When I hold my peace, then He will fight.

He will take me through, and all will be well,
As I walk in the Spirit, then all can tell
That my God will answer sincere prayer.
When you give Him praise, He will always be there

To lead and guide you through His holy Word.
If you pay attention, He will be heard
Through a still, soft voice down deep within—
As you face each challenge, the Lord will win.

So continue to praise Him with all your might,
Then you will go through each challenge, and
All will be right.

How do I respond when faced with challenges—do I turn to God in praise or retreat in fear?

ᑫ Exodus 14:14 (NIV)

"The Lord will fight for you; you need only to be still."

Reflection: This question invites you to examine your initial reactions during trials. Do you lean on God's promise to fight your battles when you choose peace and trust in Him?

Am I actively listening for God's still, small voice in my daily walk, especially during hard times?

ᑫ 1 Kings 19:12 (NIV)

"After the earthquake came a fire, but the Lord was not in the fire. And after the fire came a gentle whisper."

Reflection: The poem reminds us that God speaks in quiet moments. Are you creating space in your life to hear His whisper?

Do I use praise as a spiritual weapon when navigating life's battles?

ᑫ Psalm 34:1 (ESV)

"I will bless the Lord at all times; his praise shall continually be in my mouth."

Reflection: Praise is not only worship—it's warfare. Do you praise God consistently, even when you don't understand what He's doing?

WISDOM'S PLAN

Lord, when I need Your help each day,
You send someone with wisdom my way.
To lead and guide me with Your loving hand,
As I travel through this unknown plan.

A plan by faith You gave to me—
As I keep walking, I will surely see
That the way is made clear, just for me.
As wisdom comes—yes! It is sent by You—
I will hear and obey, and make it through.

It is not my way, my thoughts, or my plans;
I want Your purpose and Your guiding hand.
So speak to my heart in all that I do,
Father in Heaven, I love and seek You.

I want Your way, Your will, Your plan.
As I walk in Your wisdom, I am in good hands.

Am I actively seeking God's wisdom and direction in my daily life, or relying on my own understanding?

৶ Proverbs 3:5-6 (NIV)

"Trust in the Lord with all your heart and lean not on your own understanding; in all your ways submit to Him, and He will make your paths straight."

Reflection: How can you begin to lean more on God's guidance rather than your own plans this week?

How do I respond when God sends someone to guide me with His wisdom? Do I listen, pray, and obey?

৶ James 1:5 (NIV)

"If any of you lacks wisdom, you should ask God, who gives generously to all without finding fault, and it will be given to you."

Reflection: Who has God placed in your life to help guide you spiritually? Are you open to receiving that guidance?

Am I walking in alignment with God's plan, or have I been pursuing my own will over His?

৶ Jeremiah 29:11 (NIV)

"For I know the plans I have for you," declares the Lord, "plans to prosper you and not to harm you, plans to give you hope and a future."

Reflection: What specific step can you take to surrender your plans and walk more fully in His wisdom and will?

SEEING CLEARLY

Oh! How God is opening up your eyes,
To show you what is deep inside—
Of those around you, close at hand,
Who you might have thought would truly stand

For what is good, true, right, and fair,
But only gave you great despair.
To learn that years of closeness are,
Because of blood, still truly far

From what it means to give, care, and share—
But only to hold what they want
And think should be theirs.

For God has called you out to be
A great light, in which all will truly see.
The love you gave was, and is, truly rare;
You gave from your heart to all who were there.

But you will see clearly, as time goes on,
That in all this,
Your God has made you very strong.

How has God used disappointment or broken relationships to reveal His deeper purpose for your life?

ᕪ Romans 8:28 (NIV)

And we know that in all things God works for the good of those who love him, who have been called according to his purpose."

Reflection: reflect on how God may be refining your perspective and building strength in you through life's revelations.

Are you willing to release people or expectations that hinder your growth in Christ, even if they are close to you?

ᕪ Mark 3:35 (NIV)

"Whoever does God's will is my brother and sister and mother."

Reflection: Consider how spiritual family and purpose may sometimes require distance from familiar but unfruitful connections.

How can you remain a light and love others, even when you feel unseen or misunderstood?

ᕪ Matthew 5:16 (KJV)

"Let your light so shine before men, that they may see your good works, and glorify your Father which is in heaven."

Reflection: Think about how God is still using your heart and your testimony to impact others, even if they don't always acknowledge it.

DAY BY DAY

Within your life, you know His ways,
For He has been with you — **day by day**.
Throughout your life, He is always there,
To help you when you're in despair.

With all your heart, you love Him so,
But there are **some things** you must let go.
For God has led you, day by day,
Even when you went astray.

His loving-kindness, mercy, and grace
Are always there to take the place
Of problems and feelings that stood up tall —
For **God's holy power has conquered them all**.

Just let Him fix it — and fix it, He will!
And peace will abide... and all will be still.

What areas of your life are you still holding on to instead of releasing to God?

᎙ Proverbs 3:5–6

"Trust in the Lord with all your heart and lean not on your own understanding; in all your ways submit to Him, and He will make your paths straight."

Reflection: Are there burdens, habits, or emotions you need to surrender so God's peace can fill those places?

How have you seen God's mercy and grace sustain you through difficult times?

᎙ Lamentations 3:22–23

"Because of the Lord's great love we are not consumed, for His compassions never fail. They are new every morning; great is Your faithfulness."

Reflection: Can you recall specific moments where God's daily presence brought you comfort, even when you felt lost or unworthy?

Are you allowing God's peace to lead your decisions, or are you still trying to fix things in your own strength?

᎙ Philippians 4:7

"And the peace of God, which transcends all understanding, will guard your hearts and your minds in Christ Jesus."

Reflection: What would it look like today to fully trust God to "fix it," as the poem says, and let His peace take over?

CARING

Your heart is filled with love and caring,
Always giving, always sharing.
Thinking of others is what you do best,
Always working without much rest.

Blessed abundantly you will always be,
From the crown of your head to the soles of your feet.
For God has seen your life and its struggles,
And all you have given will soon be doubled.

Do not be dismayed or be in despair—
Believe, He is working things out, just because He cares.
He will lead you and guide you in all you do,
For His grace and mercy is always standing with you.

How can we continue to show Christ-like care and compassion, even when we feel unnoticed or exhausted?

◊ Galatians 6:9 (ESV)

"And let us not grow weary of doing good, for in due season we will reap, if we do not give up."

Reflection: reflect on moments when caring for others feels draining. How can God's Word and promises renew your strength?

In what ways has God demonstrated His care and provision in your life during times of struggle?

◊ 1 Peter 5:7 (NIV)

"Cast all your anxiety on Him because He cares for you."

Reflection: Share or journal a moment when you gave sacrificially, and God met your needs in return.

How can we trust God's timing for the reward of our faithful giving and serving?

◊ Luke 6:38 (NIV)

"Give, and it will be given to you. A good measure, pressed down, shaken together and running over, will be poured into your lap."

Reflection: What does this verse mean to you personally as you live a life of generosity and care?

A SITUATION FOR GOD

For in the lap of jealousy, envy, and strife,
Never look for anything to come out right.
Don't try to fight it with your own might,
For only God can win this fight.

For He will lift you and give you peace,
To place jealousy, envy, and strife under your feet.
For the hand of God is always at hand,
To lift your spirits and help you to stand,
With joy, love, peace, and rest,
You will walk in love and receive God's best.

So be encouraged, always look up, and never let go,
For the Great I Am has taken over.
Don't you see?
Don't you know?
So walk in love and always be true,
To the Spirit of God that lives in you.

"For God is your strength."
"In love."

How can we rely on God's strength and peace when facing situations filled with jealousy, envy, or strife?

◌\ Philippians 4:6-7

"Do not be anxious about anything, but in every situation, by prayer and petition, with thanksgiving, present your requests to God. And the peace of God, which transcends all understanding, will guard your hearts and your minds in Christ Jesus."

What does it mean to "walk in love" and how can we embody this in challenging situations, as mentioned in the poem?

◌\ 1 Corinthians 13:4-7

"Love is patient, love is kind. It does not envy, it does not boast, it is not proud. It does not dishonor others, it is not self-seeking, it is not easily angered, it keeps no record of wrongs. Love does not delight in evil but rejoices with the truth. It always protects, always trusts, always hopes, always perseveres."

What does the poem mean when it says "For God is your strength"? How does relying on God's strength affect our response to conflict and difficulties?

◌\ Isaiah 41:10

"So do not fear, for I am with you; do not be dismayed, for I am your God. I will strengthen you and help you; I will uphold you with my righteous right hand."

TRUST – NO – FLESH

Within Your Word, You declared therein,
Put your trust in no man, don't trust in him.
For in God's Word, it plainly states, as a matter of fact,
That through our trials, He's got our backs.

Casting all your cares and wants on Him,
For He sees and knows what's deep within.
He's got a great plan, that we don't see,
We're being molded to what He wants us to be.

So, just stand still, in your thoughts and ways,
Just stay in the Spirit and you'll see brighter days.
Keep holding on and trust in His Word,
Not many days hence, you will be heard.

So, be encouraged! Smile! And don't look down!
Your faith, hope, and trust in your God is on good ground!

How can we learn to fully trust God during trials instead of relying on our own strength or understanding?

◌\ Proverbs 3:5-6

"Trust in the Lord with all your heart and lean not on your own understanding; in all your ways submit to Him, and He will make your paths straight."

What are some ways to cast our cares on God and surrender our worries to Him, as described in the poem?

◌\ 1 Peter 5:7

"Cast all your anxiety on Him because He cares for you."

In what areas of your life are you still relying on your own strength instead of trusting God's plan? How can you let go and trust Him more fully?

◌\ Isaiah 55:8-9

"For my thoughts are not your thoughts, neither are your ways my ways," declares the Lord. "As the heavens are higher than the earth, so are my ways higher than your ways and my thoughts than your thoughts."

TRUST ME

Keep your eyes ahead of you, and never side to side
For straight ahead is where I am and where my love abides.
So, as you go from day to day through whatever task,
Always keep looking up and don't forget to ask!

Seek my divine guidance in all you do and say,
For in your life you will see, I have made the way.
Trust me and be patient and stand firm on my Word,
Yes, all things are possible no matter what you've heard.

Look to me for all you want, and every daily care,
For when you trust me, I will soon be there.
My love is everlasting and my Word is true,
I just want you to trust me, and I will bring you through.

How do you maintain your focus on God and keep your eyes ahead of you, especially during difficult times?

◎\ Proverbs 4:25

"Let your eyes look directly forward, and your gaze be straight before you."

What does it mean to seek God's guidance in all you do, and how do you practice this in your daily life?

◎\ James 1:5

"If any of you lacks wisdom, let him ask of God, who gives to all liberally and without reproach, and it will be given to him."

How can you develop greater patience and trust in God's timing and plans for your life?

◎\ Isaiah 40:31

"But those who wait for the Lord shall renew their strength; they shall mount up with wings like eagles; they shall run and not be weary; they shall walk and not faint."

CONFIDENCE IN GOD

When you ask Him, ask in faith, standing on His Word,
With confidence in your heart, knowing you have been heard.
He will open a door for you to walk through,
All things will be easy, cause it is just for you.

They will run after and chase you, your blessings that is,
All because your Father in Heaven has claimed you as His.
So, always praise Him for His wondrous acts,
For His is Alpha and Omega, you know that's a fact.

Give Him glory and honor as you go through each day,
Knowing in your heart and spirit, He will always make a way.
So, as your blessings come and call you by name,
Your confidence in God knows, He made the way.

How can you strengthen your confidence in God's ability to provide for your needs, even when circumstances seem uncertain?

⟲ Philippians 4:19

"And my God will meet all your needs according to the riches of his glory in Christ Jesus."

What are some practical ways you can stand firm in faith and trust in God's plan, especially when facing challenges or obstacles?

⟲ 2 Corinthians 5:7

"For we live by faith, not by sight."

How does recognizing God as the Alpha and Omega strengthen your understanding of His sovereignty and control over your life?

⟲ Revelation 1:8

"I am the Alpha and the Omega," says the Lord God, "who is, and who was, and who is to come, the Almighty."

THAT PLACE IN YOUR HEART

There is a place within your heart I would really like to see,
I would like to look deep down inside and see if I see me.
I want to know your thoughts, your ways, and your many cares,
When you let me in, I would gladly meet you there.

A place of sensitivity, compassion, love, and passion too,
I know it is all locked inside that special place in you.

How open am I to allowing God to see the deepest parts of my heart, and how can I invite Him into the spaces I may have kept hidden?

◌\ Psalm 139:23-24

"Search me, O God, and know my heart; test me and know my anxious thoughts. See if there is any offensive way in me, and lead me in the way everlasting."

What role does sensitivity, compassion, and love play in my relationship with others, and how can I cultivate these qualities more intentionally?

◌\ Colossians 3:12-14

"Therefore, as God's chosen people, holy and dearly loved, clothe yourselves with compassion, kindness, humility, gentleness, and patience. Bear with each other and forgive one another if any of you has a grievance against someone. Forgive as the Lord forgave you."

What does it mean to you personally to have a "special place" within your heart that God can dwell in, and how can you make space for Him there daily?

◌\ Revelation 3:20

"Here I am! I stand at the door and knock. If anyone hears my voice and opens the door, I will come in and eat with that person, and they with me."

CHANGING YOUR NAME

It's not that I don't like your name
I'd like to change it just the same
There is nothing wrong with it I must say!
But on occasion I'd like to change it anyway

Yes, I'm asking and I hope that it's ok
Cause Babe is what I really want to say
Not always you see, just from time to time
When it is appropriate, and it hits my mind

I think it is a nice name, just between you and me
So, with your consent, Babe is who you will be
It is such a small change, just a four-letter word
But in it and through it my heart can be heard!

What does it mean to you when God changes your name, as He did with Abram to Abraham (Genesis 17:5)? How can this transformation reflect God's intentions for your life?

ᆨ Genesis 17:5

"No longer will you be called Abram; your name will be Abraham, for I have made you a father of many nations."

How do you feel about the idea of God calling you by a new name, one that reflects His love and purpose for you? How can this impact your relationship with Him?

ᆨ Revelation 2:17

"Whoever has ears, let them hear what the Spirit says to the churches. To the one who is victorious, I will give some of the hidden manna. I will also give that person a white stone with a new name written on it, known only to the one who receives it."

How does showing affection through small gestures, like using a special name, reflect God's love and care for you? In what ways can you demonstrate God's love in your relationships?

ᆨ 1 John 4:7-8

"Dear friends, let us love one another, for love comes from God. Everyone who loves has been born of God and knows God. Whoever does not love does not know God, because God is love."

BE PATIENT WITH ME

Within my heart, I wish you could see
The places of pain inside of me.
Oh yes, you are right, I'm afraid you see,
Even though I'd like you inside of me.

I must go slow and take my time,
To see if you are really mine.
I want to share my heart with you,
And even spoil you through and through.

I hope I'm not too forward with this,
There is a lot in me, oh! More than just a kiss.
But time will tell, it will tell what's true,
If I can entrust my heart to you.

So, please be patient, be patient with me,
For in time, in time, we will surely see
How much the bond is between me and you.
We must trust God; He will see us safely through.

Oh yes, it will be great, me and you!

How can patience in relationships reflect God's love for us?

ᐯ James 5:7

"Be patient therefore, brothers, until the coming of the Lord. See how the farmer waits for the precious fruit of the earth, being patient about it, until it receives the early and late rains."

What does it mean to entrust your heart to others, and how does trust in God's timing shape this process?

ᐯ Proverbs 3:5-6

"Trust in the Lord with all your heart, and do not lean on your own understanding. In all your ways acknowledge him, and he will make straight your paths."

How can we cultivate patience in our relationships while allowing God to guide us through the process of trust and healing?

ᐯ Romans 12:12

"Rejoice in hope, be patient in tribulation, be constant in prayer."

REAL THOUGHTS
(In My Imagination)

Yes, there are times when I am alone,
Within my thoughts, I see—
I imagine things within my mind,
Special times between you and me.

For now, for now, that is all I have,
Yet patient I must be.
I'd rather spend more time,
Really get to know you—don't you see!

I understand, I understand, it's not quite the best time,
But it does not stop the desire
And thoughts within my mind.

So, I will be patient,
Yet longings deep within,
For time—more time—for you and me to spend.

Spending special time together
Would let us truly see,
If my imagined special thoughts can happen...
Between You and Me.

Are you inviting God into your thoughts and imagination, trusting Him with your desires?

℘ Psalm 37:4 (NIV)

"Take delight in the Lord, and he will give you the desires of your heart."

℘ 2 Corinthians 10:5 (NIV)

"We take captive every thought to make it obedient to Christ."

Reflection: How can you align your inner desires and longings with God's will for your life?

How do you practice patience and trust in God's timing for relationships or special connections?

℘ Romans 8:25 (NIV)

"But if we hope for what we do not yet have, we wait for it patiently."

℘ Ecclesiastes 3:1 (NIV)

"There is a time for everything, and a season for every activity under the heavens."

Reflection: What areas of your life is God asking you to be patient in right now?

Are you building a relationship (with God or others) on a foundation of mutual understanding and sincerity?

℘ Romans 12:9 (NASB)

"Let love be without hypocrisy. Abhor what is evil; cling to what is good."

℘ Ecclesiastes 4:9-10 (NIV)

"Two are better than one... If either of them falls down, one can help the other up.

Reflection: How can you be intentional about building godly, honest connections that honor both God and others?

GUARDING ONE'S HEART

There is always a chance—a chance you take,
When it comes to your heart... making a painful mistake.
When the scales are unbalanced on one side or the other,
One must guard their heart as they go further.

The red flags—yes! Red flags go up on every side,
You look and see them, and inside pretend to hide.
You tell yourself it will be airtight, alright it will be!
Because you miss being loved and truly can't—no, you don't want to see.

You must slow down and guard your heart,
Before you get hurt and other things start.
So, trust in the Lord and His promises to you!
He will lead and guide and take you through.

Yes, it is a difficult time and place to be in,
But you must step back—look and listen from within.
Step back, step back, and listen to that inner voice,
Then you can go forward and make the right choice.

Why is it important to guard your heart, especially when emotions are involved in relationships?

◊ Proverbs 4:23 (NIV)

"Above all else, guard your heart, for everything you do flows from it."

Reflection: How have you seen the condition of your heart affect your decisions or direction in life?

What are some "red flags" or warning signs God may use to protect you from emotional or spiritual harm?

◊ John 16:13 (ESV)

"When the Spirit of truth comes, He will guide you into all the truth..."

Reflection: Are you actively listening for the Holy Spirit's guidance when navigating close relationships?

How can trusting God's timing help you make wiser choices in love and relationships?

◊ Psalm 27:14 (KJV)

"Wait on the Lord: be of good courage, and he shall strengthen thine heart: wait, I say, on the Lord."

Reflection: In what ways can patience protect your heart and keep you aligned with God's will?

WHERE DO I FIT

Tell me, tell me—if you can!
Where do I fit in your great plan?
Am I a toy, or just some passing fling?
Or am I important in the scheme of things?

My heart is involved, you know that's true!
Tell me, tell me... am I for you?
I'm not just a fill-in to pick up the slack—
I'm in your corner; you know that's a fact!

So let me down easy or pick me up and run...
Just imagine the possibilities—oh, what fun!

Have I sought God to understand my true place in His plan?

◖ Jeremiah 29:11 (NIV)

"'For I know the plans I have for you,' declares the Lord, 'plans to prosper you and not to harm you, plans to give you a hope and a future.'"

Reflection: How can I rest in the truth that God has a specific, meaningful role for me in His divine plan?

Am I looking to people for affirmation more than to God?

◖ Galatians 1:10 (NIV)

"Am I now trying to win the approval of human beings, or of God? Or am I trying to please people? If I were still trying to please people, I would not be a servant of Christ."

Reflection: Do I value God's view of me above how others treat or define me in relationships?

Am I trusting God with my heart, or trying to fit in where I don't belong?

◖ Proverbs 3:5–6 (NIV)

"Trust in the Lord with all your heart and lean not on your own understanding; in all your ways submit to Him, and He will make your paths straight."

Reflection: Am I truly allowing God to lead me to relationships and spaces where I am seen, valued, and purposed according to His will?

HIS TOUCH OF LOVE

Sometimes we must encourage ourselves, when no one is around,
Even if they are around, no encouragement is found.
Just like King David long, long ago,
He spoke encouragement to himself when he was low.

Sometimes you feel you are all alone, with no help in sight—
That is the time to strengthen your faith with all your might.
You must remember and never forget: we are not alone.
Jesus sits high and looks low from His place upon His throne.

We must merely ask His help, and submit our will and all our cares,
Then, with confidence, knowing His love is always there.
He will touch you—He will touch you with His finger of love!
Then you will feel and know your deliverance came straight from above.

He will touch you! He will touch you! I know it's true!
His love, joy, and peace will touch you—
And make you brand new.

When have you had to encourage yourself in the Lord, like King David did?

ᕽ 1 Samuel 30:6 (KJV)

"But David encouraged himself in the Lord his God."

Reflection: How can you strengthen your faith when others are unable or unwilling to encourage you?

Do you believe God's love is always present, even when you feel alone?

ᕽ Hebrews 13:5 (KJV)

"...For He hath said, I will never leave thee, nor forsake thee."

Reflection: What scriptures or experiences remind you that Jesus is always near, even in hard times?

How have you experienced the renewing touch of God's love in your life?

ᕽ Psalm 51:10 (KJV)

"Create in me a clean heart, O God; and renew a right spirit within me."

Reflection: What does it look like for God's love, joy, and peace to make you "brand new"?

AN OVERCOMER

To overcome is what we do with Jesus in our lives!
No matter what we do or say, in Him we must abide.
So, through God's grace and mercy and never-ending care,
His love is everlasting and always will be there.

No matter what the problem, we will make it, because He loves us so!
He will take us by the hand and lead us where to go.
We must be obedient and willing, casting all our cares on Him—
He will take... and mend every one of them.

Casting out all doubt and fear and walking in great faith,
You soon will be an overcomer, in that desired place.
So, as you walk in victory and praise Him from your heart,
You will see that God sustained you, right from the start.

I am an overcomer! An overcomer I am!
Yes, I realize this is just a part of God's great plan.

What does it mean to be an overcomer in Christ, and how do I embrace that identity daily?

◌ 1 Corinthians 15:57 (NIV)

"But thanks be to God! He gives us the victory through our Lord Jesus Christ."

Reflection: How do you walk in the victory that Christ has already won for you? Are there areas of your life where you struggle to see yourself as victorious?

How can obedience and surrender to God help me overcome the struggles I face?

◌ 1 Peter 5:7 (NIV)

"Cast all your anxiety on Him because He cares for you."

Reflection: What burdens are you holding on to that God is asking you to release? How can obedience open the door to healing and strength?

In what ways can I remain faithful and praise God even in the midst of my trials?

◌ James 1:2–3 (NIV)

"Consider it pure joy, my brothers and sisters, whenever you face trials of many kinds, because you know that the testing of your faith produces perseverance."

Reflection: How does praising God through adversity shape your spiritual resilience and testimony as an overcomer?

SHARED LOVE

I am here to share and give back to you
Some of the love you've shared your whole life through
Do not think it strange, just only rare
That, there are some folk who really care

Just accept it, and thank your God above
For from only him, can come that kind of love
An everlasting love from god's own heart
That is there to help you, when things fall apart

So just keep on smiling, and always be true
To that golden heart that's been placed inside of you
Your blessings are coming, yes! they're on their way
Just pray, and give God the glory, everyday

How can we actively share God's love with others, especially when we may feel overlooked or unsupported?

᠙ 1 John 4:19

"We love because he first loved us."

What does it mean to "keep on smiling" and "always be true" to the love God has placed in our hearts, especially during difficult times?

᠙ Romans 5:3-4

"Not only so, but we also glory in our sufferings, because we know that suffering produces perseverance; perseverance, character; and character, hope."

How does God's everlasting love help us when we feel like things are falling apart?

᠙ Romans 8:38-39

"For I am convinced that neither death nor life, neither angels nor demons, neither the present nor the future, nor any powers, neither height nor depth, nor anything else in all creation, will be able to separate us from the love of God that is in Christ Jesus our Lord."

L-O-V-E

True love, comes straight from the heart,
Created by God, right from the start.
To be shared and given with no strings,
True love can conquer many things.

Sometimes misused, and tossed aside,
But, regained strength and takes in stride.
All of life's many challenges tossed at its' side,
It refuses defeat, and looks for the best.

Always stands tall, to meet every test,
It is rarely found, but when found must be cherished.
Without it, some lives have already perished.
So, we must seek to have it, and never let go,
For only true love comes from God, "Did you know?"

He will give you His love, which is constant and true,
He will always stand tall inside of you!

What does true love look like, and how does God's love for us influence the way we express love to others?

◌\ 1 John 4:7-8

"Dear friends, let us love one another, for love comes from God. Everyone who loves has been born of God and knows God. Whoever does not love does not know God, because God is love."

In the poem, it says true love refuses defeat and always stands tall. How can we demonstrate this kind of resilience and strength in our love for others, especially during difficult times?

◌\ Romans 8:37

"No, in all these things we are more than conquerors through him who loved us."

The poem emphasizes the importance of cherishing true love, which comes from God. How can we actively seek and cherish God's love in our lives, ensuring that we don't let go of it?

◌\ Jeremiah 31:3

"I have loved you with an everlasting love; I have drawn you with unfailing kindness."

A LOVING GOD

God made us, so that Him we must trust,
He created us to share, His love that none can compare.
And all we need to do is receive it and follow through,
In His Word that is our guide, there is no escape, no place to hide.

Only, to be covered with His blood and under the shadow of His wings,
We will find salvation and peace in all that He brings.
He made us all for Him, it's easy, just ask Him in,
And within your heart and soul, He will stay.

But, you must trust Him and let Him have His way,
Yes, He will help you through,
All of life's challenges set before you.
Just try Him, just trust Him, and you will surely see,
That new creature inside, you were always destined to be.

He will create in you a new heart, mind, and soul,
A true miracle will take place, when He takes control.

"Remember, He is always here waiting to love you."

How does trusting in God's love, as described in the poem, influence your daily walk of faith?

୧\ Proverbs 3:5-6

"Trust in the Lord with all your heart and lean not on your own understanding; in all your ways submit to him, and he will make your paths straight."

The poem mentions that God covers us with His blood and under the shadow of His wings. How does understanding God's protection give you peace in difficult times?

୧\ Psalm 91:4

"He will cover you with his feathers, and under his wings you will find refuge; his faithfulness will be your shield and rampart."

What does it mean to you to become a "new creature" in Christ, as mentioned in the poem? How does this transformation reflect your trust in God?

୧\ 2 Corinthians 5:17

"Therefore, if anyone is in Christ, the new creation has come: The old has gone, the new is here!"

ABBA ALL I NEED IS YOU

(As I look Back)

Throughout my life, as I look back
You were always there, and that's a fact
My life has had some ups and downs
But in each challenge, your love is found

You and your Angels protected, and kept me safe
From all hurt, harm, and danger in every place
As I look back to yester-year
All twists and turns are pretty clear

You kept and preserved me for this Great Day
When I would walk in your purpose, all the way
To stand on your Word with Patience and Faith
And be in Obedience in a Humble place

I love you Lord and you love me!
Just hold me, and keep me where you want me to be!

How have you experienced God's protection and love during times of difficulty, as described in the poem?

◌\ Psalm 34:18 (ESV)

"The Lord is near to the brokenhearted and saves the crushed in spirit."

What does it mean to stand on God's Word with patience and faith, as mentioned in the poem? How can you apply this in your own life?

◌\ 2 Corinthians 5:7 (NIV)

"For we live by faith, not by sight."

In what ways can you be more obedient to God's purpose and trust Him to guide you, as the poem emphasizes?

◌\ Proverbs 3:5-6 (NIV)

"Trust in the Lord with all your heart and lean not on your own understanding; in all your ways submit to him, and he will make your paths straight."

ABOUT THE AUTHOR

Florentine Shirley is a devoted woman of God whose life reflects her deep love for the Lord and His Word. Rooted spiritually in the African Methodist Episcopal Church, Florentine draws strength from her faith and the encouragement she first received within her church community. Her passion for ministry flows through every aspect of her life as she faithfully uses the gifts God has given her—whether through singing songs of praise, teaching, or writing heartfelt poetry that brings comfort, peace, love, and joy to others. Her words often reach those who are in transition, facing challenges, or simply in need of a friend.

Florentine's life of service extends far beyond the church walls. She has faithfully served at **The Good Samaritan Hospital for over 50 years,** where she was recently honored for her outstanding longevity and invaluable contributions. Her presence has been a beacon of compassion and dedication to both staff and patients alike.

In addition to her professional and spiritual service, Florentine is a **Board Member of Vessouls of Transformation Sisters of Change**, a nonprofit organization committed to empowering women and teens in their life journey and purpose. Her involvement in this mission reflects her unwavering belief in encouraging and uplifting others, especially women, through God's love and wisdom.

A loving mother and grandmother, Florentine is the proud parent of two sons and the joyful grandmother of a grandson and a granddaughter. Her life continues to be a beautiful testimony of grace, purpose, and unwavering faith—a true vessel of transformation in her family, community, and beyond.

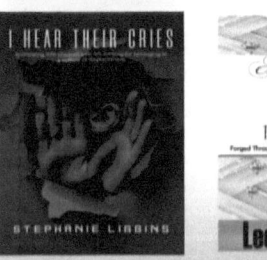

www.ingramcontent.com/pod-product-compliance
Lightning Source LLC
Chambersburg PA
CBHW031229120626
46545CB00003B/1046